PLANET NEPTUNE IS BLUE!

ASTRONOMY FOR KIDS
CHILDREN'S ASTRONOMY BOOKS

Speedy Publishing LLC

40 E. Main St. #1156

Newark, DE 19711

www.speedypublishing.com

Copyright 2017

All Rights reserved. No part of this book may be reproduced or used in any way or form or by any means whether electronic or mechanical, this means that you cannot record or photocopy any material ideas or tips that are provided in this book.

If you look at an image of the planet Neptune, you will see that it is blue! Is it all water? Let's find out!

THE OTHER BLUE PLANET

Earth, from space, looks like a blue planet because our oceans cover so much of the planet's surface.

Neptune is another "blue planet" in our solar system, but it is so far from the warmth of the Sun that any water it has is hard-frozen. Instead, the blue color comes from the way Neptune's atmosphere reflects the Sun's light.

EARTH AND NEPTUNE

URANUS

Neptune's neighbor Uranus is a lighter blue, and we do not yet know what other material in Neptune's atmosphere is responsible for the deeper color.

The atmosphere of Neptune is mainly hydrogen, methane and helium. Fragments of frozen methane in the atmosphere absorb the red spectrum of the Sun's light, and reflect back light in the blue spectrum. It looks like a welcoming ocean world, but as it turns out Neptune is a lot less comfortable than that.

4,498,396,441 km (30.10 AU)

ATMOSPHERE
Hydrogen 80%
helium 19.0%
methane 1.5%

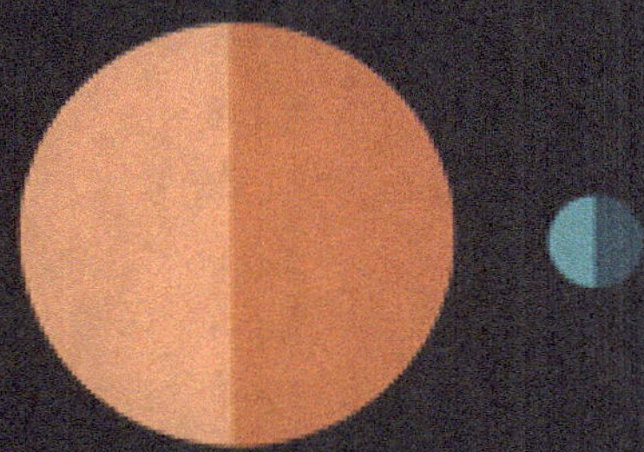

Neptune size compared to Earth

Temperature

GETTING TO KNOW NEPTUNE

Neptune is the furthest planet in our solar system, beyond the other gas giants Jupiter, Saturn, and Uranus. Gas giants are huge, massive balls of gas with a relatively small rocky core.

NEPTUNE

GAS GIANT PLANETS

This is different from planets like Mars and the Earth, which are rocky balls with a comparatively thin atmospheric layer. (Read about the Earth's atmosphere in the Baby Professor book *A Shield Above Us*.)

The mass of Neptune is seventeen times the mass of Earth, and it is the planet with the second strongest gravitational pull in the solar system. It is thirty times further away from the Sun than the Earth is, although when it was forming it may have had an orbit much closer to the Sun.

SOLAR SYSTEM

NEPTUNE

Neptune orbits very quickly on its axis: despite it being so large its day is only sixteen Earth hours long. However, it is so far out from the Sun that Neptune takes over 164 Earth years to make a single orbit. In fact, in 2011 Neptune finished its first orbit since it was discovered in 1846. You could say we have known of the planet for a single Neptune year!

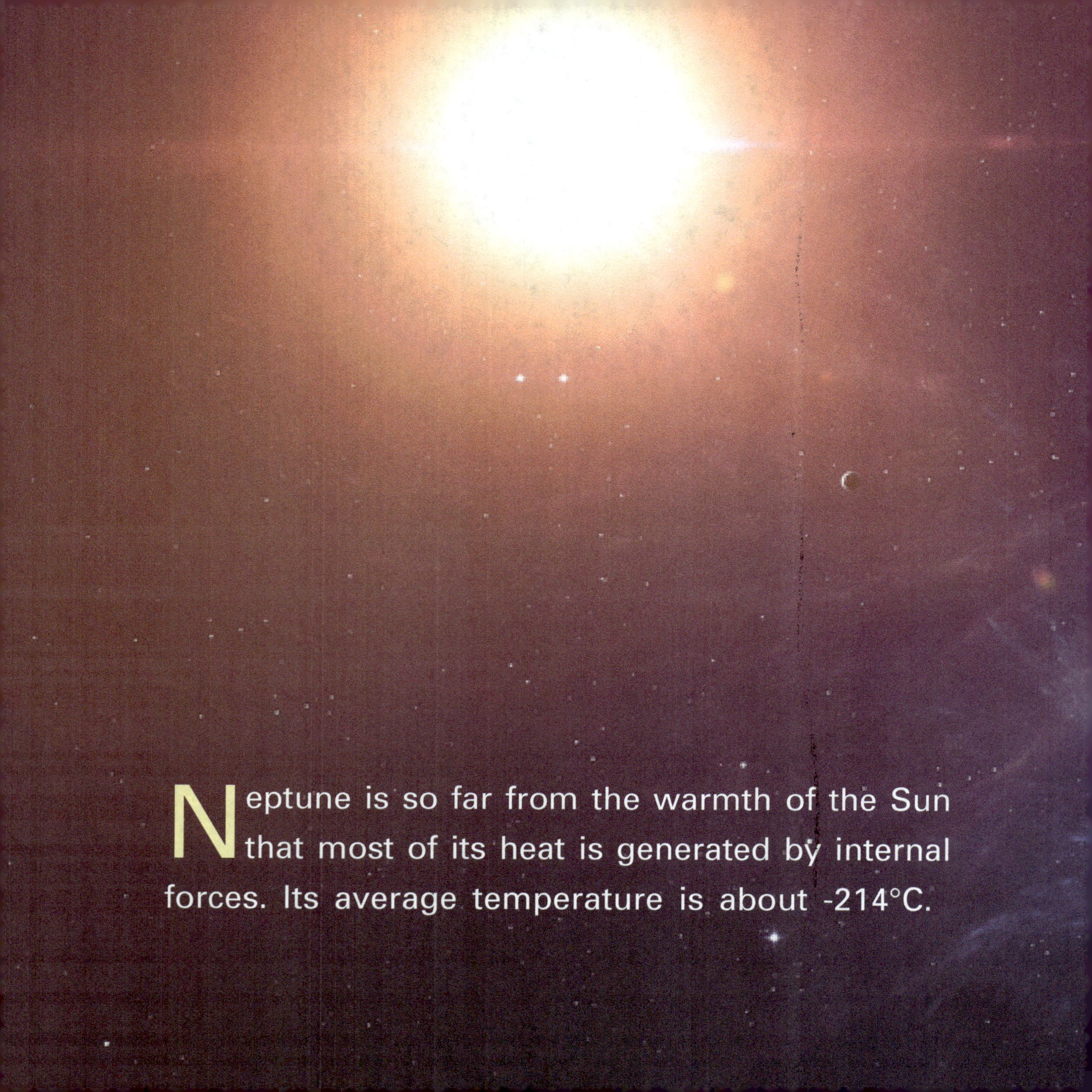

Neptune is so far from the warmth of the Sun that most of its heat is generated by internal forces. Its average temperature is about -214°C.

DISCOVERING NEPTUNE

Although early astronomers and students of the skies knew about most of the other planets in ancient times, they did not know about Neptune because it cannot be seen from the surface of the Earth by the naked eye.

ANCIENT ASTRONOMER

WILLIAM HERSCHEL
A BRITISH ASTRONOMER WHO DISCOVERED URANUS

The planet Uranus, Neptune's neighbor, was discovered in 1781. Soon after that scientists noticed that its orbit was irregular, as if it were being pulled at by some other massive object. The most likely source of the pull was another large planet even further away from the Sun.

By studying the variations in the orbit of Uranus, astronomers were able to work out where this other large planet was likely to be. Then they knew where in the sky to start searching for it.

Uranus And Neptune

Finally, in 1846, Urbain le Verrier of France and Johann Galle of Germany managed to capture Neptune by telescope. They relied on the calculations of astronomer John Couch Adams, which he had published in 1845.

URBAIN LE VERRIER

JOHANN GALLE

NEPTUNE'S ATMOSPHERE

Neptune's atmosphere is extremely thick. It is about 75 percent hydrogen and almost 24 percent helium, with the last bit being mainly methane.

The atmosphere has icy clouds, and Neptune's winds reach the highest speeds of wind anywhere in the solar system.

NEPTUNE

The upper atmosphere of Neptune is hazy, with a sort of smog of "snowflakes" of hydrocarbons.

The flakes melt as they fall toward the surface of the planet and experience higher pressure closer to the ground.

Scientists have recorded two interesting weather patterns in the atmosphere of Neptune:

- **Dark Spots**. In 1989 the Voyager 2 space craft made a fly-by of Neptune on its way out of the solar system. It sent back images of huge storms causing dark areas in the atmosphere.

These storms are like the more famous Great Red Spot on the planet Jupiter; however, the Great Red Spot has been raging for hundreds of years, while the Dark Spots were gone when the Hubble Space Telescope started studying the planet in 1994.

DARK SPOT IN THE ATMOSPHERE OF NEPTUNE

"SCOOTER" ON NEPTUNE

- **Scooter**. Voyager 2 also noted a fast-moving storm system that scientists called Scooter. It was much smaller than the Dark Spots, and was white against the background blue of the atmosphere.

As well as being divided into an upper and lower layer, Neptune's atmosphere is divided into "bands" around the planet, like different stripes on a Christmas ornament. In some of the layers, the winds reach record speeds.

INNER STRUCTURE ELEMENTS OF NEPTUNE

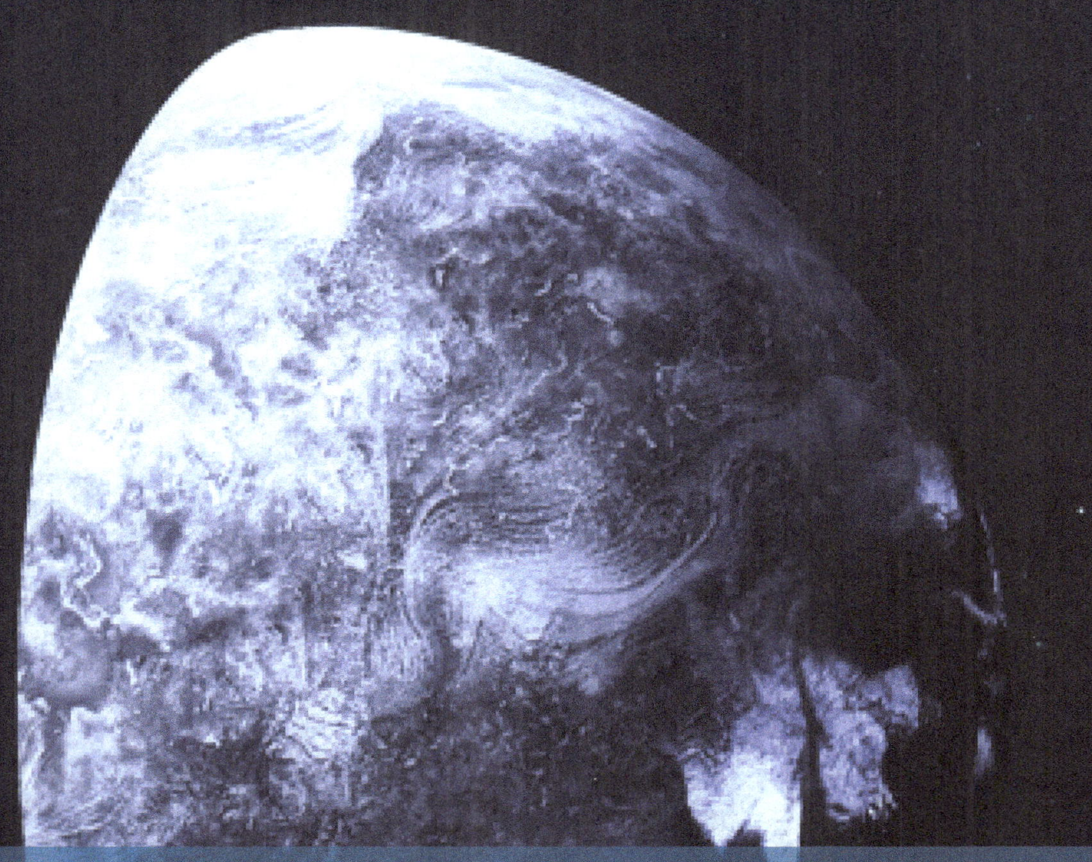

BELOW THE ATMOSPHERE

The small solid center of Neptune has two layers:

CORE
7500 km
MANTLE
10.500 km
ATHMOSPHERE
7500 km

- **The core**. The center of the planet is rocky, and denser than Earth's core.

- **The mantle**. Around the core is a layer of dense, hot liquid, a mix of water, methane and ammonia. The mass of the mantle of Neptune is about 15 times the mass of our entire Earth.

Neptune emits more than twice the heat that it receives from the Sun. This generation of heat from the center of the planet may be what provides the power for the immense winds in the atmosphere. This is a difference from Uranus, which emits almost exactly the same amount of heat as it receives from the Sun. The solid center of Neptune rotates quickly, like those of Jupiter and Saturn. This gives the planet a day of about sixteen hours.

ike the Earth, Neptune is slightly tilted in relation to its orbit around the Sun. The planet experiences "summer" and "winter" as its north pole tilts either toward or away from the Sun, but of course these seasons are radically different from what we experience on our planet.

NEPTUNE AND ITS MOONS

IN ORBIT AROUND NEPTUNE

Neptune has at least fourteen moons, some of them orbiting at great distances from the planet. The largest and most interesting of the moons is *Triton*. Astronomers discovered Triton just a few weeks after confirming the existence of Neptune in 1845. However, they just called it "the satellite of Neptune" until the 1940s, when more of Neptune's moons were discovered. Once there was more than one, each moon got its own name.

It is a frozen moon that has a thin atmosphere of its own. Geysers of dust and frozen nitrogen shoot out of the interior of Triton, rising as high as five miles above the surface before sinking back down. The surface of the moon is complex, with huge areas that seem to have been melted alongside areas of rougher and more jagged terrain and fields of craters where other objects have struck the moon. The melted areas may be a result of when Neptune captured Triton: the gravitational forces involved in the capture may have liquified the moon, and Triton might have stayed liquid, or at least soft, for as much as a billion years.

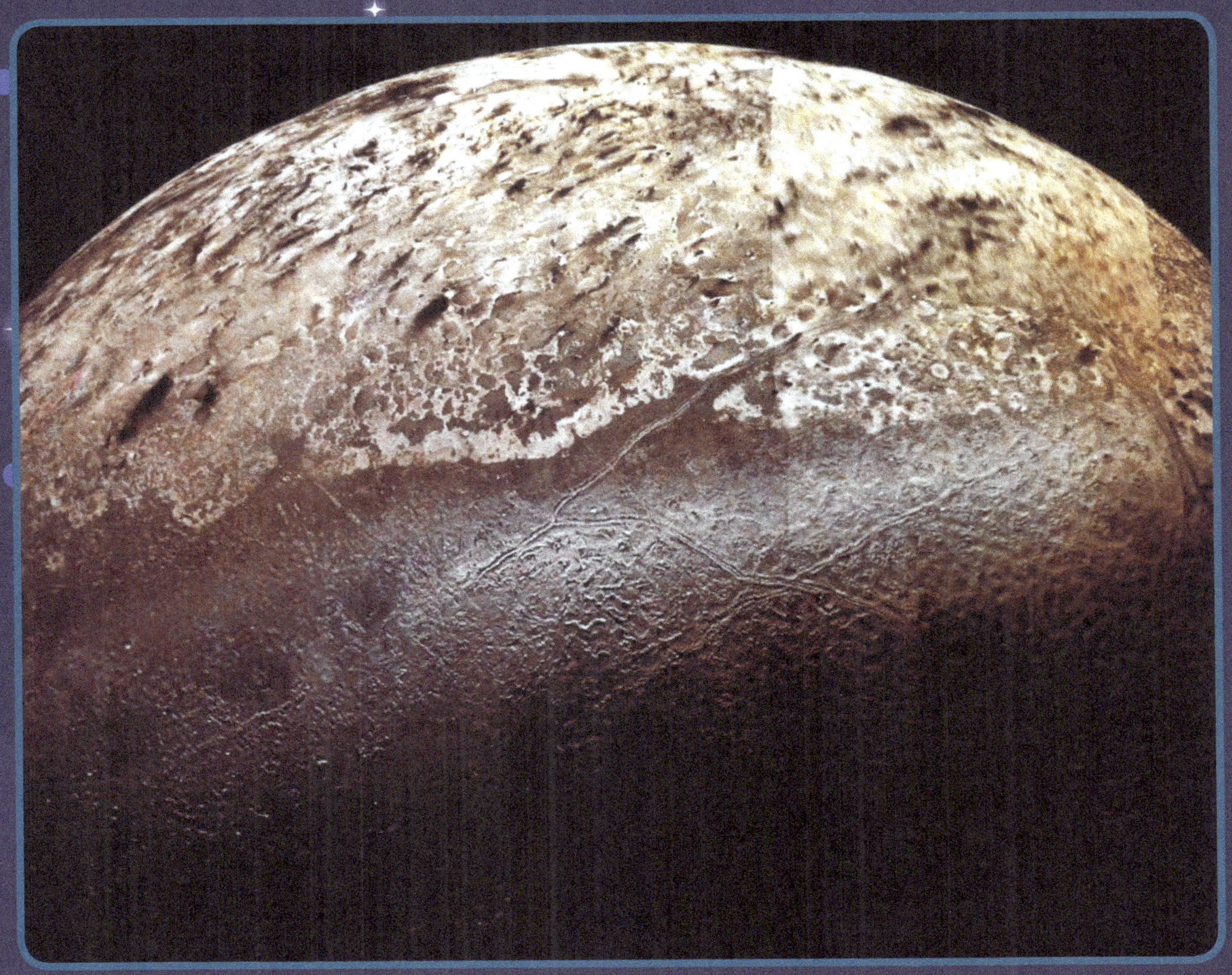

TRITON MOON

Triton orbits Neptune in the opposite direction from the planet's rotation, which means it may have started out as an object deeper in space, in the Kuiper Belt.

It may have been caught by Neptune's gravitational field well after the moon developed, as the path it was traveling intersected the orbit of Neptune.

Triton is possibly the coldest place in the solar system, with a surface temperature around -235ºC.

NEPTUNE'S RINGS CAPTURED BY VOYAGER 2 1989

Neptune also has several faint *rings* made up of a combination of ice particles and dust. Some sort of carbon-based mixture probably coats the particles. The rings are very faint, unlike the rings of Saturn. The Voyager 2 fly-by in 1989 provided the first good views of the rings, and the first confirmation that they were complete rings around the planet, and not just partial rings of orbiting debris.

NEPTUNE FUN FACTS

Here are some things to know about Neptune:

- As with most of the planets, Neptune is named after a Greek god. In this case, it is the brother of Zeus who ruled the oceans of the world.

- Although Neptune is smaller than Uranus, its neighbor gas-giant planet, Neptune has a much greater mass.

When Voyager 2 visited Neptune, it recorded data from its onboard sensors and took pictures. It had to send the data and images home to us because Voyager 2 was on a one-way trip out of the solar system. The spacecraft provided the only close-up images that we have of the planet, although the Hubble Space Telescope and other telescopes have since added to our stock of pictures of Neptune. The distance from us to Neptune is so immense that the signals Voyager 2 sent home took more than four hours to arrive at Earth.

LEARN OUR NEIGHBORHOOD IN THE UNIVERSE

We are traveling through space on the planet Earth, warmed by the Sun and protected from many of the dangers of space by the atmosphere around us. Humans have been as far as our own Moon, and we have sent out space craft like Voyager 1 and Voyager 2, but no people have traveled further than our Moon so far. One day people will get to other planets in our solar system, and perhaps even beyond!

Learn more about what lies beyond our atmosphere, and how we might visit our neighbors in the solar system, in Baby Professor books like *Where Does Outer Space Begin?*, *Is our Moon the Only Moon in the Solar System?*, *What is an Astronaut?* and *A Space Ride to Saturn*.

Visit

BABY PROFESSOR
EDUCATION KIDS

www.BabyProfessorBooks.com

to download Free Baby Professor eBooks
and view our catalog of new and exciting
Children's Books

www.ingramcontent.com/pod-product-compliance
Lightning Source LLC
Chambersburg PA
CBHW080803120726
48001CB00009B/2837